IF YOU DIE TOMORROW

A Simple Guide to Estate Planning

Michael A. Lilly

**A member of the California and Hawaii
State Bar Associations.**

First Edition 1990
Second Edition 1994
Third Edition 2004
Library of Congress Card Number 93-151693
ISBN 0 - 9640614 - 0 - 6

This book is not intended to provide specific legal advice regarding the reader's estate. The author disclaims liability for any losses incurred from the use, directly or indirectly, of any information in this book. The reader is cautioned to seek the advice of an attorney, qualified tax advisor or accountant before taking any action or making any decisions about his or her estate.

Although the persons and events described herein are hypothetical, they are based on actual cases and are representative of the most common legal and factual issues and questions handled by estate-planning attorneys.

Dedicated to my parents, Tony and Ginger, whose lifelong devotion to one another and support of me have been the principal inspirations of my life.

This text was printed using recycled acid-free paper.

Michael A. Lilly, Esq.

Michael A. Lilly is an estate-planning lawyer licensed to practice in the states of California and Hawaii. He graduated with honors from the University of the Pacific Law School. He is a former Attorney General of Hawaii and is an experienced trial lawyer and appellate advocate. He has five children, and is a partner in the Honolulu law firm of Ning, Lilly & Jones, 707 Richards Street, Suite 700, Honolulu, HI, 96813, Telephone: (808) 528-1100, FAX: (808) 531-2415, michael@NLJLaw.com, www.NLJLaw.com.

TABLE OF CONTENTS

C. PREPARE FOR PROBATE

D. DEATH TAX AVOIDANCE

E. DISABILITY AND DEATH WITH DIGNITY

F. CHOOSING YOUR ATTORNEY

FOREWORD

Not long ago "Felicia," a member of the "baby boom" generation, called about an estate plan for her parents.

Her mother and father were in their 70's and owned two houses: their home and a rental, together valued at $600,000.

Neither Felicia nor her parents had done any estate planning. They incorrectly thought it would cost too much and their estate was too small.

On a whim Felicia called me. It was a good thing she did. I gave her my five-minute "estate planning course." I explained how, for about $1,500 in attorneys' fees, her parents could save tens of thousands of dollars in probate costs and hundreds of thousands of dollars in potential future death taxes.

Felicia said, "I never knew estate planning was so easy and inexpensive. More people need your estate planning advice."

That gave me an idea. Many books on the market are supposed to help you plan your estate. Often, they are boringly detailed or written in unintelligible "legalese."

Some are self-help form books. I don't think it's wise for anyone to act as his own attorney. There is an old maxim: "An attorney who represents himself has a fool for a client." That goes for non-attorneys, too.

It became clear to me that what people needed was a layman's guide to estate planning. Not a how-to book, but a book which summarized the strategies used by attorneys to protect estates.

This book describes easy ways to avoid probate, reduce death taxes and get your assets to your heirs without delay.

A. INTRODUCTION

pro•bate (prō'bāt) adj. The orderly and systematic conversion of your property into attorneys fees, court costs and death taxes.

will (wil) n. A probate attorney's retirement plan.

1. DON'T PROCRASTINATE: ACT NOW!

You could die tomorrow! So don't procrastinate. Act now to avoid probate, save death taxes and transfer property to your heirs privately and without delay.

"Ted" had worried about his estate for years.

He and his wife owned a modest home, had $100,000 in their IRA and received a small retirement pension. He had done no estate planning because he feared it would cost too much and that his estate was too small. His most difficult task, like most of us, was to stop procrastinating and call an estate-planning attorney.

He learned that estate planning is easy and inexpensive. And you are never too old or too young to reduce death taxes, avoid probate costs and delays, and leave as much property as possible to your children.

That's what this book is all about. This book may be the most important estate-planning tool you have ever read.

B. PROBATE AVOIDANCE

No one in his or her right mind would intentionally allow their estate to go through probate.

2. WHAT IS PROBATE?

Probate is the expensive, time-consuming and public court proceeding that transfers your assets to your heirs after you die.

"Sheila" was a widow who owned a small condominium valued at $300,000. She had no mortgage and no other major assets. Sheila wanted to leave everything to her only daughter, "Sarah." Like many of us, Sheila had only a vague understanding of what probate was and why it should be avoided.

Probate is the court proceeding that transfers your property to your heirs after you die. Here are some of the things that happen in probate, all of which you should **AVOID:**

- A court file is opened on your estate.

- Your estate hires a probate attorney.

- Your estate hires an executor to supervise your probate proceeding.

- Your attorney and executor **each** get a statutory fee up to or more than **two- to five-percent of your estate!**

- Newspaper advertisements notify the world that your estate is being probated.

- Your assets are inventoried and appraised.

- Your heirs can contest your will.

- Because probate is public, anyone can look at your probate file.

- Your heirs may not get your assets for up to 18 months or more.

3. WHY YOU SHOULD AVOID PROBATE.

Probate costs lots of money, takes too much time, and opens your estate files to the public. There are easy ways to avoid probate.

There are four major reasons for people like Sheila to avoid probate:

- **Probate is expensive.** The executor's and attorneys' fees would cost Sheila's small estate more than $15,000!

- **Probate takes too long.** Sheila's estate would average 18 months in probate.

- **Probate is public.** Any stranger could open Sheila's probate file to learn what she owned and to whom she was leaving her property. In Oklahoma, a burglar used probate files to target heirs of valuable properties.

- **Probate encourages litigation.** Because probate is a court proceeding, anyone can easily challenge her will in probate. Thus, probate invites litigation.

No one in his or her right mind would intentionally allow their estate to go through probate.

The next few chapters give easy and inexpensive ways for people like Sheila and you to avoid the costs, time delays and publicity of probate.

4. WHY A TRUST CAN HELP YOU AVOID PROBATE.

A trust is an easy way for you to avoid probate and death taxes.

Like many people, Sheila believed four common myths about trusts:

- "Trusts are for the rich!"
- "Trusts are complicated!"
- "Trusts are expensive!"
- "Trusts take away control of my property!"

False! False! False! False!

- **Trusts are for everyone.** Trusts were at one time mainly used by the wealthy. Today, nearly everyone should use them.

- **Trusts are simple.** A trust is normally as simple to prepare as an ordinary will.

- **Trusts are inexpensive.** An average probate can cost 10-15 times the cost of a trust. The question is not whether you can afford a trust, but whether you can *afford not to have* one to protect your estate.

- **A trust keeps you in the driver's seat.** Because you dictate every condition of your trust, you have control of your trust.

There are many types of trusts. The next few pages explain the most common trusts used to protect property from probate and death taxes.

5. WHAT IS A TRUST?

A trust is a way to entrust a person or organization with property for the benefit of any person or organization.

One of the most common questions I am asked is, "What is a trust?"

Simply defined, a trust is a way to entrust a person or organization with property for the benefit of a person or organization.

For example, a person can set up a trust for himself (*e.g.*, a revocable living trust), a charity (*e.g.*, a charitable remainder trust) or family members (*e.g.*, irrevocable family trust). A person can also set up a trust to last only for a specific period of time (*e.g.*, grantor retained income trust) or for grandchildren (*e.g.*, a generation-skipping trust).

Anyone can set up a trust. Any kind of property can be placed in a trust. Property can remain in a trust for as short a time as you want or almost indefinitely.

As the next chapters will show, you can set up a trust which you are free to change or one which is unchangeable. You can also set up a trust during your life or through your will.

All living trusts have one thing in common: they avoid probate.

REVOCABLE TRUST:
CHANGEABLE

- Avoid costs
- Avoid publicity
- Avoid delays

- Avoid costs
- Avoid publicity
- Avoid delays
  AND
- Avoid death taxes

IRREVOCABLE TRUST:
UNCHANGEABLE

6. TRUSTS ARE REVOCABLE OR IRREVOCABLE.

*Trusts are either **revocable** (changeable) or **irrevocable** (unchangeable). Both are easy ways to avoid probate.*

A revocable trust is **REVOCABLE**—you can revoke or change it anytime you wish. Its primary purpose is to avoid the costs, publicity and time delays of probate.

An irrevocable trust is **IRREVOCABLE**—once you set it up you can never change it. It not only avoids probate, but it also can avoid death taxes and capital gains taxes.

LIVING TRUST:

**TRUST
SET UP
DURING
YOUR
LIFE.**

TESTAMENTARY TRUST:

**TRUST
SET UP
AFTER
DEATH.**

7. TRUSTS MAY BE CREATED DURING LIFE OR BY WILL.

*Trusts are either **living** (set up during your life) or **testamentary** (set up by your will). A living trust avoids probate; a testamentary trust does not.*

A living trust is set up during your life. You also transfer your property into the living trust during your lifetime. Its primary purpose is to avoid the costs, publicity and time delays of probate.

A testamentary trust is set up by your will. Your testamentary trust does not receive any assets until after your death. It can avoid capital gains and death taxes, but it does not avoid probate.

A REVOCABLE LIVING TRUST IS A WAY FOR YOU TO HAVE YOUR "ESTATE" CAKE AND EAT IT TOO.

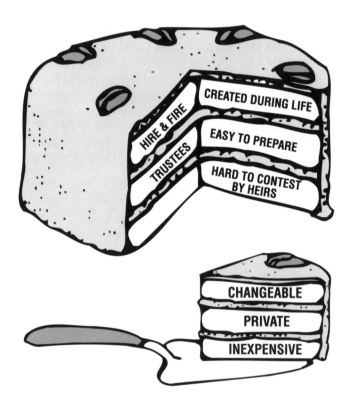

8. REVOCABLE LIVING TRUSTS AVOID PROBATE.

A revocable living trust is an easy way to avoid probate and to quickly and privately transfer your assets to your heirs.

Because a revocable living trust is revocable, you can change it any time you want. You can put property into the trust and you can take it out. You can change the beneficiaries and what you want them to receive.

A revocable living trust has other benefits.

- Avoids the costs and delays of probate.
- Allows immediate transfer of assets to heirs.
- Protects minor children.
- Protects incompetent or spendthrift heirs.
- Ensures privacy.
- Is more difficult to contest than a will.
- Allows professional management.
- Ensures no disruption of affairs after death.
- Is easy and inexpensive to prepare.
- Can avoid death taxes.

TYPICAL APPOINTMENT OF
SELF AS TRUSTEE

*The following is a typical provision appointing
yourself as your own trustee.
You can name any adult
as your trustee.*

THIS TRUST AGREEMENT is made this

_____day of _____, 19___,

between COSMO PEACOCK, of the State
of Hawaii, as settlor, and COSMO
PEACOCK, as trustee (hereinafter referred
to as the trustee).

As you can see, it is easy to appoint you or anyone else
as the trustee of your revocable living trust.

9. NAME A TRUSTEE OF YOUR TRUST.

Your trustee is the person you choose to manage your trust. Often, it's you.

"**C**osmo Peacock" wondered if he had to hire a trust company to be the trustee of his revocable living trust.

The answer is, "NO!" Any adult can be your trustee.

My clients normally choose themselves or family members to be their trustees because:

- You can usually "trust" yourself or a family member with your property.

- It is less expensive for you or a family member to manage your trust than to hire a professional trustee (see Chapter 10).

I also recommend you name one or two or more successor trustees, usually your spouse, child, best friend and/or a trust company to carry out the instructions in your trust if you become mentally or physically incapacitated or die.

Some clients prefer to name several co-trustees, including themselves. Often, one of the co-trustees is a professional trustee or trust company.

10. NEGOTIATE YOUR TRUSTEE FEES.

When you choose a professional trustee or trust company as your trustee, shop around and negotiate your fees.

"**J**ill" set up a trust and hired a trust company to manage her affairs as her professional trustee. She was led to believe the law required her to pay an expensive statutory trustee fee.

Not so. Every state has a trustee fee statute. Most states allow a trustee to charge:

- One to five percent of the income from your trust.

- One to two percent of the value of any property you remove from your trust.

NO LAW SAYS YOU CANNOT NEGOTIATE YOUR TRUSTEE FEES!

Professional trustees and trust companies can be effective. They can also be expensive. They can and should negotiate their fees. If they refuse to negotiate, shop around.

There are many professionals who want your business.

TYPICAL BENEFICIARY PROVISION

The following is a typical trust provision naming beneficiaries. In this case, the surviving spouse inherits, but if he or she has already died, the heirs receive the estate.

IF MY SPOUSE SURVIVES ME: If my spouse survives me, then at my death the trustee shall distribute the residuary trust estate, free and clear of any trust, to my spouse.

IF MY SPOUSE PREDECEASES ME: If I am survived by any of my descendants, but not by my spouse, then at my death the trustee shall distribute the residuary trust estate, free and clear of any trust, among my descendants living at my death, *per stirpes**, as follows:

Jane	50 percent
Jonathon	50 percent

*per stirpes, see Chapter 38.

11. NAME BENEFICIARIES OF YOUR TRUST.

A revocable living trust is just like your will. You can name your beneficiaries and what you want them to receive from the trust.

Many people think of a revocable living trust as a "will substitute."

Why? Because, just like your will, the beneficiaries of your trust are the heirs of your estate.

Your trust names your heirs and what you want them to inherit from your estate when you die.

Usually, a revocable living trust leaves a person's estate to his or her surviving spouse. The trust usually names other beneficiaries, such as one's children, if his or her spouse has already died. Typical examples of these provisions appear on the next page.

But remember. Everyone needs a will. See Chapter 20.

TYPICAL TRUST SCHEDULE
TRANSFERRING PROPERTY

The following is a typical schedule attached to a revocable living trust transferring personal property to the trust:

Schedule A

The following is a description of the original assets of the JOHN JONES REVOCABLE LIVING TRUST.

1. Cash: _____.

2. All of my jewelry, wearing apparel, personal effects, furniture, furnishings, rugs, books, papers, pictures, prints, paintings, objects of art, silverware, china, glass, linens, other household effects and supplies, and all other unregistered tangible personal property of whatsoever description and wheresoever situated.

12. TRANSFER PROPERTY INTO YOUR TRUST.

A **revocable living trust** *is just an empty shell until you put property into it. You can easily transfer any property into your trust.*

"**A**nnie Jones" and her late husband, "John," made a very expensive mistake. They had prepared their own self-help revocable living trusts to avoid the time and costs of probate.

Yet, after her husband died, Annie learned that all his property was going to go through probate. And their children were eventually going to be hit with an unnecessary death tax. See Chapter 42.

Why? Because Annie and her husband failed to do the most important thing of all: transfer their assets into their trusts.

Any property—from cash to real estate—can be put in your trust. For example:

- You can attach a list transferring cash and personal property into your trust (a typical schedule appears on the prior page).

- Your attorney can deed your house to your trust.

- Your broker can transfer stocks to your trust.

- Your bank can transfer your accounts to your trust.

Remember, funding your trust is as important as setting it up in the first place.

HOW TO PROTECT YOUR ESTATE
FROM FIFI LAMOUR

STEP ONE:
Set up an irrevocable
family trust.

STEP TWO:
Place your property
into the trust, either
during your life
or by your will.

IRREVOCABLE
FAMILY TRUST

STEP THREE:
The trust provides your
surviving spouse with
income for life.

FAMILY
TRUST

STEP FOUR:
After your surviving
spouse dies, your
property goes
to your heirs.

FIFI LAMOUR
LOSES

13. IRREVOCABLE FAMILY TRUSTS AVOID PROBATE.

An irrevocable family trust is an easy way to avoid probate, to provide lifetime income to your surviving spouse and to ensure your heirs and not the "other" spouse inherits your property.

Joan asked, "How do I protect my property from Fifi Lamour?"

"Who is Fifi Lamour?" her attorney replied.

"Oh, I made her up. She's some hussy who will be after my husband and my property after I die. I want to make sure my property goes to my children and not to Fifi Lamour."

"You need an irrevocable family trust," she was advised.

There are three major benefits of an irrevocable family trust:

- It avoids probate.

- For a married couple with an estate up to $1.2 million or more, it saves death taxes. See Chapters 47 and 48.

- It makes it **impossible** for Fifi Lamour to get her hands on your property.

An "anti-Fifi Lamour provision" (which lawyers call a QTIP) can prevent the next spouse from disinheriting your children. See Chapter 61.

WHAT HAPPENS TO JOINT, ENTIRETY & COMMON PROPERTY

The following chart shows what happens to your property after your death if held jointly, as tenants by the entireties or as tenants in common.

Jointly:	As tenants by entireties:	As tenants in common:
Your half goes to other joint tenant, by-passing probate.	Your half goes to your spouse, by-passing probate.	Your half goes to your heirs.

14. JOINT OWNERSHIP AVOIDS PROBATE.

Holding title jointly is an easy way to leave your assets to the survivor and avoid probate. There are disadvantages to this strategy.

You can own property in two basic ways: tenancy in common; and joint tenancy.

The difference between the two has to do with what happens at death.

A tenant in common's interest in the property passes to the heirs, normally through probate. However, a joint tenant's interest passes immediately to the surviving joint tenant, bypassing probate.

Joint tenancy by a married couple is called tenancy by the entireties. When one spouse dies, the survivor inherits one half the property free of probate.

Joint tenancy used to be popular because it avoids probate. However, most estate planning attorneys don't recommend joint ownership any more because:

- IT DOES NOT avoid death taxes.
- IT DOES NOT avoid probate upon the death of the surviving joint tenant or if you both simultaneously die in a common accident.
- IT DOES NOT protect your property from a new spouse (Fifi Lamour, see Chapter 13) if your surviving spouse remarries.

There are more effective ways to avoid probate, *e.g.* by a revocable living trust.

15. LIFE INSURANCE AVOIDS PROBATE.

You can easily provide your heirs with life insurance free of probate.

So long as you do not make your own estate the beneficiary of your life insurance, the insurance is completely free of probate.

16. BANK ACCOUNT TRUSTS AVOID PROBATE.

A **bank account ("Totten") trust** *is an easy way to leave assets to your heirs free of probate.*

In most states, your bank will assist you in setting up a "bank account trust" (also known as a "Totten" trust). You have full control of the bank account for your life. After your death, it goes to your designated beneficiary completely free of probate.

17. GIFTS AVOID PROBATE.

You can easily avoid probate by making gifts to your heirs.

Any gift you make during your life, to anyone, completely avoids probate. But see Chapters 43, 44, 49 and 52 for potential gift and death taxes.

18. RETIREMENT PLAN BENEFICIARIES AVOID PROBATE.

Naming a beneficiary of your retirement plan, IRA or pension plan, completely avoids probate.

You can avoid probate by naming your heirs as the beneficiaries of your retirement plan, IRA or pension plan.

19. OTHER STRATEGIES AVOID PROBATE.

There are many other strategies available to you to avoid probate.

The foregoing are by no means the only ways available to you to avoid probate. Some of the other strategies are dealt with elsewhere in this book, but are listed below.

- Gifts during life (Chapters 43, 44 and 49).

- Grantor retained income trust (Chapter 51).

- Gift to charity (Chapter 52).

- Charitable remainder trust (Chapter 53).

- Generation-skipping trust (Chapter 56).

- Transfer by annuity (Chapter 58).

- Transfer by installment (Chapter 59).

- Sale and lease back (Chapter 60).

- Uniform Gift to Minors Acts.

You can use these and other strategies for your estate to avoid probate. Your estate-planning attorney can assist you in tailoring them for your estate.

C. PREPARE FOR PROBATE

Where there's a will, there's a way.

YOU DIE WITHOUT A WILL

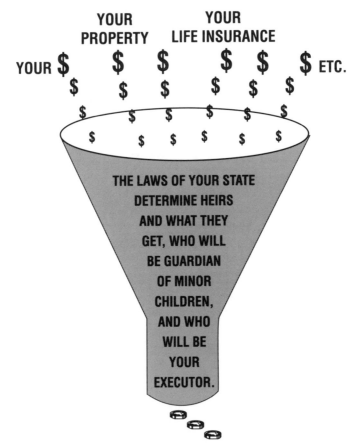

YOUR
PROPERTY

YOUR
LIFE INSURANCE

YOUR **$** **$** **$** **$** **$** **$** ETC.

THE LAWS OF YOUR STATE DETERMINE HEIRS AND WHAT THEY GET, WHO WILL BE GUARDIAN OF MINOR CHILDREN, AND WHO WILL BE YOUR EXECUTOR.

AT LEAST EIGHTEEN MONTHS LATER YOUR HEIRS GET WHAT IS LEFT OF YOUR ESTATE.

- **MINUS DEATH TAXES**
- **MINUS ATTORNEY FEES**

- **MINUS PROBATE COSTS**
- **MINUS EXECUTOR'S FEES**

20. WHAT IF YOU DIE INTESTATE — I.E., WITHOUT A WILL?

If you die without a valid will and leave property outside your trust or not in joint tenancy, the laws of your state will determine who gets your property.

Nearly every week a new client or a caller on my estate planning radio show asks, "All my property is in my revocable trust or held by joint tenancy; do I need a will?"

The answer is, "Yes, yes, yes, yes, yes, yes........!"

There are three major reasons to have a will:

- Death-tax avoidance.

- Dying without a will (i.e., "intestate") is bad planning. If you leave any property without a will, the laws of your state will decide who gets your property, who will be the guardian of your minor children and who will handle your probate.

- Even with the best planning, it is nearly impossible to avoid probate. See Chapter 21.

- A will gives you control of your estate.

21. YOU CAN'T TOTALLY AVOID PROBATE.

Because it is nearly impossible to totally avoid probate, you must prepare a will.

Ideally, if you put all your property into your revocable living trust or in joint tenancy, your estate would totally avoid probate. However, we do not live in an ideal world.

Even with the best planning, some of your property just won't make it into your trust before you die because:

- You may **procrastinate** too long.

- You may **forget** to put your car in the trust.

- You may **mistakenly** believe something was put in the trust, but it was not.

- You may not have **time** to put something in your trust before your death.

- You may be **unaware** of the existence of property you inherited just before your death.

The next few chapters give easy and inexpensive ways for you to ensure the probate court follows your instructions.

TED SMART'S "INTESTATE WILL"

I, TED SMART, being of unsound and undisposing mind and having failed to make a will do hereby allow the laws of my state to determine what happens to my property.

1. Although I want my wife to have all my property, under the laws of my state I give her only 50 percent, leaving her utterly destitute.

2. I give my children 50 percent of my property, even if they are still minors.

    a. If my children die before me, I give my parents 50 percent of my property, even if they don't need the money and my wife does. If my parents die before me, I give my brother and sister 50 percent of my estate, even though it never occurred to me they would get anything of mine.

    b. I have an adopted child who I wanted to disinherit, but since I failed to make a will, it's OK if the child gets part of my estate.

3. If my children are minors, I want my estate to hire an expensive lawyer to ask a court to appoint a guardian, who can be anyone chosen by the court. I really want my brother to be the guardian. He is responsible and loves my children. However, I forgot to name him. It's OK with me if the guardian is my sister, who is an irresponsible spendthrift. It doesn't matter that she will control my property until my children reach 18.

4. I don't name an executor. It's OK with me if a stranger controls my estate.

5. I don't "pour-over" any of my property into a trust because I never set one up. It doesn't bother me that my estate will be socked with huge and unnecessary probate costs and death taxes.

6. I don't care if my wife's next husband winds up with everything I own. It's OK with me if my children become disinherited because of my stupidity.

IN WITNESS WHEREOF, I have elected not to have a will because I want to encourage people to fight over my property and to leave my family with a financial nightmare.

22. WHY YOU NEED A WILL.

A will is an easy way to direct who will inherit your property, administer your estate in probate, and be the guardian of your minor children.

"Ted" had five children, one of whom was a minor. His wife had died several years ago. He wanted his brother, not his sister, to administer his estate and to be his minor child's guardian. And he wanted to disinherit two of his older children.

Under the laws of Ted's state, if he died without a will (*i.e.,* "intestate"), all five children would share his property equally and his sister *might* be appointed guardian of his minor child and administrator of his estate.

Because Ted did not execute a will, none of his wishes were carried out. His "Intestate Will" is illustrated on the prior page.

A will could have provided the following, all of which are discussed in the next few chapters:

- named the guardian of his minor children.

- named the executor of his estate.

- avoided the "unnamed" child.

- "poured-over" his property to his trust.

- discouraged will contests with a no-contest clause.

A properly prepared will is valid in every state.

23. CHOOSE THE GUARDIAN FOR YOUR MINOR CHILDREN.

Your will allows you to name who you want as the guardian of your minor children.

Ted wanted his brother and not his sister to be the guardian of his minor child.

If he died without a will, anyone — a stranger or his sister or his brother or the state — could petition the courts to be appointed guardian. The court determines who that will be.

Ted wanted his brother Jim to raise his minor child because Jim had always loved the boy. Ted did not want his sister, Jane, to raise his son because she had never cared for the child.

There are plenty of examples of the "Janes" getting the child and control of the child's assets. Why? Because the "Teds" neglected to name their brothers as guardian in their wills!

A will is an easy and inexpensive way to choose the guardian of your minor child. Ask your attorney to include a clause naming alternate guardians if your primary guardian dies or is unable to serve.

24. CHOOSE THE EXECUTOR OF YOUR ESTATE.

Your will allows you to choose the executor of your estate in probate.

Ted wanted his brother and not his sister to be the executor of his will — *i.e.*, the person to administer this estate in probate.

If he died without a will, anyone — a stranger or his sister or his brother or the state — could ask the courts to be appointed his executor. The court determines who it will be.

Ted wanted his brother Jim to handle the estate because he had always been a very responsible person. Ted did not want his sister Jane to handle his estate because she had never been a very responsible person.

There are many examples of "Janes" becoming the executor. Why? Because Ted neglected to make it known in his will he wanted Jim to be executor!

A will is an easy and inexpensive way for you to choose the executor of your estate. Ask your attorney to include a clause naming alternate executors if your primary executor dies or is unable to serve.

TYPICAL DISINHERITANCE CLAUSE

The following is an example of the language used in Jack's will disinheriting his adopted daughter, Rosey.

I give One Dollar ($1.00) to my adopted daughter, ROSEY SMITH, if she survives me. I declare this bequest is intentional and not occasioned by accident or mistake, it being my intention that the bequest of One Dollar ($1.00) be her sole share of my estate.

25. WHAT IF YOU DON'T NAME A CHILD?

If you neglect to mention a natural, adopted or illegitimate child in your will or trust, the child may get more of your estate than you wanted.

"**J**ack" was in his 70's and had a simple estate plan. He wanted to leave all his property to his three natural children.

After his will was prepared, he was again asked, "You're sure you have no other children?"

He paused and replied, "Well — uh — over 40 years ago I adopted Rosey Smith, the daughter of my first wife. But I haven't heard from Rosey since the 1940's. I don't want her to get anything — so let's just not mention her."

In most states, if you fail to specifically mention a natural, adopted or illegitimate child in your will, the law presumes you forgot to include the child. It is called a "pretermitted child." Such a child can break the will and get a percentage of your estate.

Jack's will was changed to disinherit Rosey by leaving her $1.

TYPICAL "POUR-OVER" WILL PROVISION

The following is a typical "pour-over" will provision.

I give all the remainder of my estate and any property over which I may possess any power of appointment by Will or otherwise, to the trustee then acting under that certain Trust Agreement of even date herewith, heretofore executed by me as settlor, to be added to and become a part of the trust estate created thereby and to be held, administered, and distributed under such Agreement as amended prior to my death. I direct that such trust shall not be administered under court supervision, control, or accounting, and the trustee shall not be required to give bond in such capacity.

26. "POUR-OVER" YOUR ESTATE TO YOUR TRUST.

You can easily "pour-over" your property from your will to your living or testamentary trust.

Think of your will and your revocable living or testamentary trust as two pots. Now think of the property outside your trust as a liquid. A "pour-over" provision allows you to "pour" the property from your will to your trust after your death.

Why have a "pour-over" provision? As I mentioned earlier, it is nearly impossible to ensure that all your property will get into your trust. This device will guarantee all your property winds up in your trust.

WHEN YOU FAIL TO INCLUDE A SIMULTANEOUS DEATH CLAUSE:

Mr. & Mrs. Powers die without a simultaneous death clause. Who gets the estate?

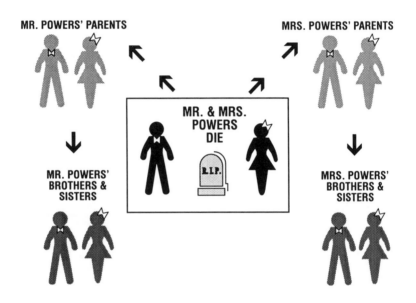

- If the probate court rules that Mr. Powers died first: Mrs. Powers' parents get the entire estate. If her parents are already dead, Mrs. Powers' siblings get the entire estate.

- If the probate court rules that Mrs. Powers died first: Mr. Powers' parents get the entire estate. If his parents are already dead, Mr. Powers' siblings get the entire estate.

27. WHAT IF YOU AND YOUR SPOUSE DIE IN THE SAME ACCIDENT?

A "simultaneous death" clause in your will permits you to identify which spouse died first, if you and your spouse die in the same accident.

Common calamities proved troubling before the use of the "simultaneous death" clause. Without such a clause, it was difficult, if not impossible, for the probate court to determine which spouse died first in a single, common accident.

"So what?" you ask. It is immensely important to know who died first to determine who will ultimately inherit the estate.

For one example, consider the "Powers," a childless husband and wife who executed mutual wills, leaving their entire estate to the surviving spouse. Assume they died in a one-car accident. If the probate court determines the husband died first, the wife's surviving parents or siblings would inherit the entire estate. However, if the probate court determines the wife died first, then the husband's surviving parents or siblings would inherit the entire estate. The potential heirs each hired attorneys and experts to fight over which side would inherit the estate.

To ensure your desires are carried out and to minimize controversies between your potential heirs, it is vital to include a simultaneous death clause in your will.

TYPICAL NO-CONTEST CLAUSE

*The following is a typical no-contest clause
used in a will or trust:*

If any heir-at-law of mine, as determined under the laws of the state of my death relating to descent and distribution of property, objects to any provision herein or directly or indirectly engages in any contest in connection with this [will] [trust], I hereby specifically disinherit that heir-at-law and further direct that such person will be cut off from any share whatsoever in my estate and I further direct that any bequest heretofore made by me to that heir-at-law will be considered as part of my residuary estate.

28. HOW YOU CAN DISCOURAGE WILL CONTESTS.

A no-contest clause discourages disappointed heirs from suing your estate for more than you gave them in your will.

"**H**oward" had four children. He wanted to leave 50 percent of his estate to his only daughter and the remaining 50 percent to his other three sons. He was worried, however, that the three sons would contest the disproportionate distribution of his estate.

It was simple to include a "no-contest clause" in his will. The clause stated that any beneficiary who challenged the will would be disinherited. The clause does not prevent challenges, but it highly discourages them.

29. SAFEGUARD YOUR WILL.

*Place your will in a safe location and tell
your family where to find it.*

"**J**im" wanted to disinherit some beneficiaries, appoint a new guardian of his minor children, choose a new executor of his will and make some major changes to his estate plan.

Jim had a new will drafted which revoked his old one. However, he did not destroy all copies of his old will. After Jim died, no one knew about the new will and his heirs only found the old one.

What happened to Jim's estate? It could not be proven that Jim had revoked the old will with a new one. Therefore, his estate was probated under the old will and none of his changes were carried out.

You must ensure your will is safeguarded and that members of your family know where to find your will when you die. Some clients leave a copy in their attorney's safe deposit box. I prefer they not put their wills in their own safe deposit boxes because they might be sealed upon their deaths.

TYPICAL REVOCATION CLAUSE

*The following is a typical clause
revoking prior wills:*

I, JOHN DOE, currently domiciled in the State of Hawaii, being of sound and disposing mind and memory, hereby declare this to be my Last Will and Testament and revoke all Wills or Codicils heretofore made by me:

30. HOW YOU CAN AVOID REVOCATION CONFUSION.

There are some easy ways for you to avoid confusion over whether your prior wills were revoked.

Jim created confusion over whether he created a new will and whether his old will had been revoked. As a result, he lost control over his own estate and his plans were not carried out.

To avoid situations like Jim's from happening to you:

- Have your new will revoke all prior wills.

- **Destroy** all copies of your old will before witnesses (preferably ones who are likely to outlive you).

- **Tell your witnesses** it is your intention to revoke your old will.

- Place your will in a safe place. See Chapter 29.

- **Tell your family** where to find your new will.

31. WHY YOU SHOULD AVOID CODICILS.

A "codicil" is a document which amends your will. It is often used in emergencies. The best practice is to draft a new will.

You can amend your will any time you want. A "codicil" is a document which amends any part of your will. For example, you can change a bequest from one heir to another or add beneficiaries. It must be executed with the same formalities as your will.

A codicil is very useful in an emergency. For example, if you are leaving on a trip and want to change part of your will, a codicil may be the answer for you.

I do not recommend codicils except in emergencies because of the problems they can create. If a codicil becomes lost, your change may never be known. If you do not follow all the legal formalities of executing a valid will, the codicil may be ruled invalid. Sometimes a codicil can create confusion, especially if there is a mistake in the codicil about which provision of your will it is intended to amend.

Drafting a codicil normally costs about the same as drafting a new will. All of the wills I draft for my clients are on computer. Thus, for me it is easier to print out a new will with the changes than adding a codicil.

32. WHAT IS AUTOMATIC, STATUTORY REVOCATION?

Under the laws of many states, your will is automatically revoked by remarriage, divorce, death of a beneficiary, etc. Periodically update your will to avoid this pitfall.

Since he executed his old will, "George" and his wife had divorced. However, George still wanted to leave 50 percent of his estate to his ex-wife, the other 50 percent to two of his children and to disinherit an adopted child. He incorrectly decided it was unnecessary to prepare a new will.

Under the laws of George's state, **his will was automatically revoked** upon his divorce. The probate court determined that he had died "intestate" — *i.e.*, as if he had no will. His ex-wife was not entitled to anything from his estate and his three children — including the adopted child — inherited everything equally.

This expensive result could have been avoided if George had sought the advice of an attorney. He would have learned that under the laws of many states, wills are automatically revoked upon certain events, such as remarriage, divorce, the birth of a child, the death of a beneficiary, etc.

33. WHAT ARE STATUTORY RIGHTS OF INHERITANCE?

In most states, your spouse and minor children can't be disinherited from receiving a minimum percent of your estate in probate.

Many states entitle the surviving spouse and minor children to a minimum percentage of your estate. If you choose to leave them less than the statutory minimum, they have a right to claim the difference from your estate.

There are, however, some exceptions. They may not be able to claim any of your estate in your revocable living trust. See your estate-planning attorney regarding the laws of your state on automatic rights of inheritance.

34. WHAT IF YOU DON'T PROVIDE FOR YOUR SURVIVING SPOUSE?

In most states, if you die without a will your children automatically inherit a percentage of your estate. If you want to provide more than the statutory amount to your spouse, you must state your wishes in your will.

"**F**red" incorrectly assumed that the laws of his state provided that his wife "Gloria" would inherit his entire estate. He decided not to write a will.

It was a costly error for his wife. Under the laws of his state, Gloria was entitled to only one third and their two minor children two thirds of his property. **He left Gloria with an estate nightmare.**

Gloria discovered she had to file an expensive petition to become the court-monitored guardian of her two minor childrens' share of Fred's estate. After each child reached majority — 18 years of age — Gloria was required to give them their share of Fred's estate.

Under the laws of most states, if you die without a will, your spouse and children are automatically given a set percentage of your estate. If you wish to provide more than the statutory percentage to your surviving spouse, you must state your wishes in your will.

TYPICAL WITNESS FORM

The following is a typical form used in a state requiring three witnesses.

Signed, published, and declared by PAT SMITH, as and for her Last Will and Testament, in the presence of us, all being present at the same time, who at her request, in her presence, and in the presence of each other have hereunto signed our names as witnesses on the date above written, and we certify that Pat Smith is in our opinion and belief of sound and disposing mind and memory.

_____
JANE DOE, Witness

_____
JOHN DOE, Witness

_____
RICHARD ROE, Witness

35. WHAT IF YOUR WILL IS NOT PROPERLY WITNESSED?

Under the laws of your state, your will must be witnessed by a minimum number of adults (usually two or three). Failure to have it properly witnessed can invalidate your will.

"Pat Smith" used a self-help will kit to prepare her will. She used two witnesses, one of whom was a minor, to sign her will. She was unaware that the laws of her state required three **adult** witnesses. Her will was held invalid and the laws of her state determined who would receive her estate.

Before executing a will, review with an attorney the unique requirements of the laws of your state regarding qualifications and minimum number of witnesses.

36. IS A WILL EXPENSIVE?

*A properly-prepared will is an inexpensive
way to guarantee your wishes
are carried out.*

Pat used a self-help will kit because she wanted to save on attorneys' fees. Yes, it was inexpensive to buy the kit. But the results were disastrous. Her failure to properly prepare her will under the laws of her state resulted in a legally invalid will. She died intestate, which was very costly to her estate.

It is very easy to fall into an estate-planning trap. As in the case of Pat, the mistake is usually not discovered until too late — after death. **I suggest you not become one of the estate "horror stories."**

Unfortunately, too many people put off having a will prepared or resort to cheap will kits because of an erroneous belief that it costs too much to have one prepared by an attorney.

In fact, wills are generally very easy and inexpensive to prepare. Attorneys charge anywhere from $100-$500 for a will, depending on the complexity of the estate. That is inexpensive insurance which guarantees your wishes are carried out.

37. WHY AVOID ORAL, HANDWRITTEN, VIDEO & STATUTORY WILLS.

Avoid the pitfalls of oral, handwritten, video and statutory wills. Have your attorney prepare a time-tested normal will for you.

You can prepare an orthodox (normal) or unorthodox (abnormal) will.

An orthodox will is one which is drafted by your attorney and witnessed by two or three people. It is valid in every state no matter in which state it is prepared.

There are four types of unorthodox wills: oral; handwritten; video; and statutory. An oral ("nuncupative") will is made verbally, normally when death is near. A handwritten ("holographic") will is written in your own handwriting. A video will is made on camera or videotape. A statutory will is prepared on a fill-in-the-blanks form.

Only a few states allow oral, handwritten or statutory wills. No state, to my knowledge, allows a video will. Unorthodox wills have numerous potential pitfalls. If you fall into any of the pitfalls, your estate may end up being probated under the laws of your state and not according to your wishes.

Do the right thing — have your attorney prepare a time-tested and orthodox will. It is inexpensive, easy to prepare and valid everywhere.

PER STIRPES

SALLY DIES

KERRY

GETS 1/2

MOLLY (DECEASED)

GRAND-CHILD 1   **GRAND-CHILD 2**

GETS 1/4   **GETS 1/4**

PER CAPITA

SALLY DIES

KERRY

GETS 1/3

MOLLY (DECEASED)

GRAND-CHILD 1   **GRAND-CHILD 2**

GETS 1/3   **GETS 1/3**

38. SHOULD YOU LEAVE PROPERTY "PER STIRPES" OR "PER CAPITA"?

*If a child predeceases you, leaving grand-children, it is very important whether you leave your estate **per stirpes** or **per capita.***

"It's all Greek to me," said one client. At first, the concepts of **per stirpes** and **per capita** confuse most clients. Yet, they are very simple.

Per stirpes means you inherit by "right of representation," while **per capita** means you inherit in your "own right." An example, diagrammed on the preceeding page, should clear it up.

"Sally" had two children, "Molly" and "Kerry." Molly predeceased Sally, leaving two grandchildren.

If Sally left her estate to her descendents **per stirpes**, the two grandchildren would receive only what Sally had left to Molly. Sally's surviving child, Kerry, would receive one half of her estate; the two grandchildren would share Molly's one half.

If Sally left her estate to her descendents **per capita**, the two grandchildren would share equally with Kerry. Kerry and the two grandchildren would each receive one third of her estate.

Most clients want their children to share equally and thus leave their estate **per stirpes**. But it is important that your will designate whether you wish your property left **per stirpes** or **per capita**.

39. SHOULD YOU AND YOUR SPOUSE HAVE JOINT OR MUTUAL WILLS?

*A joint will is one will signed by two people.
Mutual wills are two wills with reciprocal
provisions. Both are normally used
by spouses and both have pitfalls.*

"Harold" and "Martha" had been married for many years. They wanted to leave their estates to one another. The survivor of the two would leave his or her estate to their two children.

They could execute joint or mutual wills. Wills such as these are normally prepared for married couples. A joint will is a single will signed by both spouses. Mutual wills are two wills, each with reciprocal or similar provisions.

I recommend mutual wills and not a joint will for several reasons.

- **Mutual wills are easy to prepare.** They can be easily prepared on a word processor.

- **Mutual wills are inexpensive.** Because they usually mirror one another, it costs no more to prepare two wills than one will.

- **Joint wills invite litigation.** Often, a joint will is used to protect marital assets from the survivor's second spouse. The survivor frequently attempts to break the controls imposed by the joint will.

- **Joint wills are too restrictive.** They make it difficult for the survivor to handle unforeseen future circumstances.

If you wish to restrict the ability of the survivor to dispose of your property after your death, I recommend using an irrevocable family trust. See Chapter 13. That is simpler than trying to tie the hands of the surviving spouse from the grave in a joint will.

40. WHAT ARE BEQUESTS, DEVISES AND RESIDUE?

Bequests are gifts of personal property. Devises are gifts of real estate. Residue is what is left over in your estate after all gifts are made.

We often hear about bequests, devises and residue. It is important to know the definitions of the terms so we understand the words used in our wills.

A **bequest** is normally a gift of property in your will. It can be cash, a piece of jewelry, a sofa or any other type of tangible personal property.

A **devise** is a gift of real estate in your will. It can be your house, an apartment or other real property owned by you.

Residue is what is left over in your estate after all your bequests and devises are made. Your will always describes how your heirs will share in the residue of your estate. If you fail to include a "residual clause," the laws of your state and not your wishes may decide who gets the residue of your estate.

41. HOW SMALL ESTATES CAN AVOID PROBATE.

Most states exempt small estates, usually those worth $5,000 - $20,000, from probate.

Every state has laws exempting small estates from formal probate. For such estates, all that is required is an affidavit or a very informal, uncomplicated and quick procedure.

Whether your estate qualifies depends upon the laws of your state. Some allow you to file an affidavit transferring your estate to your heirs. Others have what is called "summary probate" which allows your estate to be tranferred to your heirs easily and quickly.

Seek the advice of an attorney to determine whether your estate comes under any of your state's exemptions.

D. DEATH TAX AVOIDANCE

There are two things you can't avoid:
death and taxes.
But you can avoid
death taxes.

42. AVOID, AVOID, AVOID, AVOID DEATH TAXES.

Death taxes can eat up to 50 percent of your assets. There are some easy things you can do to avoid taxes on your estate.

Avoid, avoid, avoid, avoid, avoid death taxes. Have I repeated it enough?

The federal government and many states levy a tax on you for dying. The federal tax is known as an "estate tax." The state tax is known as an "inheritance tax." For simplicity, I refer to these taxes as death taxes.

The death tax is based on a percentage of the value of your entire estate. The tax on estates over $1 million begins at 37 percent and increases to 50 percent. The amount you can leave tax free and the death rate changes almost every year, so consult an attorney for the current rates. It is a progressive tax; the more valuable your estate, the higher the tax.

There is one obvious reason to avoid death taxes. The more you avoid, the more you leave to your heirs.

The next few chapters give easy and inexpensive ways for you to avoid death taxes.

$11,000 YEARLY TAX-FREE GIFTS

You can give $11,000 to as many people as you choose, every year, free of all gift and estate taxes.

YOU

$11K $11K $11K $11K $11K $11K $11K $11K $11K $11K $11K $11

43. GIVE $11,000 CASH TO ANYONE, GIFT- AND DEATH-TAX FREE.

You can easily give $11,000 each year to as many people as you want without paying any gift or death taxes.

The federal government and several states levy a tax on you for making a gift. It is called the "gift tax."

The gift tax is normally equal to the death tax. Any property you give to your heirs over $11,000 is subject to the gift tax. On the other hand, you can give $11,000 each year to as many people as you want without paying any taxes.

Thus, for example, a married couple can give $22,000 to each of their children without paying any gift or death taxes. Over a period of years, many families can reduce their estates substantially by making these tax-free gifts.

EXAMPLE OF THE USE OF AN
IRREVOCABLE FAMILY TRUST

PROBLEM:

The Bakers want to transfer a $200,000 apartment to five children free of gift and estate taxes and probate.

SOLUTION:

STEP ONE: The Bakers set up an irrevocable family trust with five children as beneficiaries. The children are to receive assets of the trust after their parents' deaths.

STEP TWO: The Bakers transfer $100,000 of the apartment to the irrevocable family trust free of gift and death taxes on or before December 31.

STEP THREE: The Bakers transfer the remaining $100,000 of the apartment to the irrevocable family trust free of gift and death taxes on or after January 1 of the following year.

RESULTS:

- A $200,000 apartment is out of the Baker estate in less than two days.

- No probate cost or delays.

- No gift or death taxes.

44. GIVE $11,000 OF REAL ESTATE, GIFT- AND DEATH-TAX FREE.

You can easily give $11,000 worth of real estate each year to as many people as you want without paying any gift or death taxes.

Mr. and Mrs. "Baker" owned a small rental apartment valued at $200,000 which they wanted to give to their five children.

They could deed to each of their children $22,000 worth of the apartment gift- and death-tax free every year. Because they had five children, the Bakers could therefore give away $110,000 — or 55 percent — of their interest in the apartment every year. What's more, the Bakers could transfer one-half the apartment on or before December 31 and the remaining one-half on or after January 1. **In less than two days, the Bakers could legally transfer the apartment to their children free of all taxes.**

If the Bakers wanted to restrict their children from selling the apartment until after they died, the apartment could be deeded into an **irrevocable family trust.** See Chapters 13 and 48. Once the apartment was transferred into the trust, the children would not receive title until after their parents' deaths. An example of this is described on the next page.

45. WHAT IS THE DEATH-TAX ON PROPERTY YOU LEAVE YOUR SPOUSE?

You pay no death-taxes on property you leave to your surviving spouse.

Mr. and Mrs. "Anderson" were extremely wealthy, with an estate valued at over $10 million. Assume Mr. Anderson died, leaving the entire portion of his estate — $5 million — to his wife.

How much death tax would the federal government charge his estate?

Nothing!

Fortunately, we are permitted to leave an estate of unlimited size to our surviving spouses free of death taxes. This is known as the "marital exemption."

46. WHAT IS YOUR $1 MILLION LIFETIME DEATH-TAX CREDIT?

*Anyone can leave an estate up to $1 million
to anyone not his or her spouse
free of death taxes.*

Mrs. "Barry" had an estate valued at $1 million. Her husband had predeceased her and she wanted to leave her estate to her two children free of taxes.

If her husband were alive she could leave him her entire estate free of death taxes. However, let's assume her husband had already dies and she was leaving her $1 million estate to her children.

How much death tax would the federal government charge her estate?

Nothing!

Fortunately, we are permitted to leave up to $1 million to anyone other than our spouses free of death taxes. This is known as our "lifetime death-tax credit" or "unified credit."

This exemption from death taxes is in addition to the marital exemption described in Chapter 45. Thus, you can leave an estate of unlimited size to your spouse free of death taxes and an **additional** $1 million to your children or anyone else free of death taxes.

HOW AN ESTATE OF $2 MILLION CAN LOSE OVER $400,000 IN DEATH TAXES

$2 million estate

Mr. Stuart dies

$2 million goes to Mrs. Stuart death-tax free.

Mrs. Stuart dies

$1 million goes to the children death-tax free. But her estate will pay over $400,000 on the additional $1 million.

Children

The children receive an estate of less than $1.6 million.

47. MARRIED COUPLES: LEAVE UP TO $2 MILLION TAX FREE.

A married couple can leave up to $2 million free of death taxes.

Mr. "Stuart" owned $2 million of assets which he wanted to leave to his wife. After her death, the entire $2 million would go to their children.

Under this plan, Mrs. Stuart would receive the $2 million estate free of death taxes. However, when she died, she could only leave one-half of the $2 million estate to their children tax free. They would be hit with an unnecessary death tax of over $400,000!

There are two easy ways Mr. Stuart could leave $2 million to their children tax free:

- **Option one:** Mr. Stuart could leave $1 million to Mrs. Stuart and $1 million to the children tax free. But that deprives Mrs. Stuart of the income from the $1 million for her life. See diagram on opposite page.

- **Option two:** Mr. Stuart could leave $1 million to Mrs. Stuart and $1 million in an irrevocable family trust. Mrs. Stuart would receive the income from the $1 million for life. On her death, the entire $2 million would go to their children tax free. This option is the one most people prefer. See diagram opposite Chapter 48.

HOW A MARRIED COUPLE CAN TRANSFER AN ESTATE OF $2 MILLION DEATH-TAX FREE

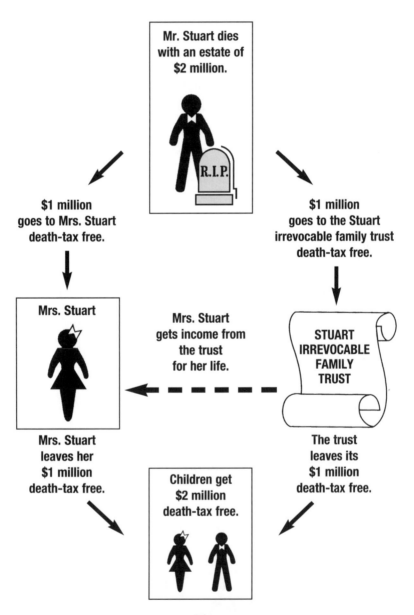

Mr. Stuart dies with an estate of $2 million.

$1 million goes to Mrs. Stuart death-tax free.

$1 million goes to the Stuart irrevocable family trust death-tax free.

Mrs. Stuart

Mrs. Stuart gets income from the trust for her life.

STUART IRREVOCABLE FAMILY TRUST

Mrs. Stuart leaves her $1 million death-tax free.

The trust leaves its $1 million death-tax free.

Children get $2 million death-tax free.

48. HOW DO IRREVOCABLE FAMILY TRUSTS AVOID DEATH TAXES?

An irrevocable family trust is an easy way to provide lifetime income to your surviving spouse and to save death taxes up to $2 million of your estate.

Mr. "Stuart" set up an irrevocable family trust. When he died, $1 million went to Mrs. Stuart and $1 million went into the trust free of death taxes and probate.

Mrs. Stuart received the income from the $1 million for life. After she died, their children received the $1 million in the trust and Mrs. Stuart's $1 million free of death taxes and probate. The opposite page shows a diagram of this strategy.

Simple? You bet!

Inexpensive? Yes!

For an investment of about $1,000 - $2,000, a $2 million estate can easily save over $400,000 in death taxes and probate costs! That's a **guaranteed return** on your investment that even T-bills can't provide. Yet, families get socked with huge and unnecessary death taxes every day.

49. HOW TO USE YOUR LIFETIME $1 MILLION DEATH-TAX CREDIT NOW.

You don't have to wait for death to use your lifetime death-tax credit. You can give up to $1 million during your life to your heirs free of death and gift taxes and probate.

Mr. "Smith" was in his 70's, had five children and expected to live another 13 years or more.

He owned rapidly appreciating real estate worth $400,000 in a prime commercial location. The property was expected to increase substantially — to $1 million — within 10 years.

How could he transfer the property to his children without paying too much death or gift taxes?

One strategy available to him was to use part of his lifetime death tax credit during his lifetime instead of waiting until after his death.

Under this strategy, Mr. Smith could give the $400,000 property to his children now. Because he could credit the gift against his $1 million lifetime death tax credit, he would pay no death or gift taxes. He would still have an additional $600,000 lifetime death tax credit available to him. He would avoid probate on the property. And, most importantly, by the time of his death the property would have greatly appreciated free of any additional taxes.

50. WHY PAY THE GIFT TAX ON APPRECIATING PROPERTY NOW?

You can easily reduce death taxes by paying the gift tax on appreciating property now.

Mr. "Smith" also could have given the income-producing property outright to his five children today. With their $11,000 per person per year gift tax exemption, $55,000 of the gift would be tax free.

Mr. Smith would pay a gift tax on $345,000. But the expected increased value of the property — $600,000 — would go to his children entirely free of probate and death taxes!

The gift ultimately could save Mr. Smith's estate thousands of dollars in death taxes and probate costs.

51. GRANTOR RETAINED INCOME TRUSTS AVOID DEATH TAXES.

A grantor retained income trust is an easy way to reduce death taxes and avoid probate on rapidly appreciating property.

Another alternative for Mr. Smith would be to place the income-producing property in a grantor retained income trust ("GRIT").

What is a GRIT?

No, it's not a breakfast food. It is a trust into which the Smiths could put their income-producing property for up to 20 years. They would receive the income from the property for 20 years, after which the property would be transferred to their five children.

There are at least four major benefits of a GRIT:

- Mr. Smith would receive income from the property for 20 years.

- Gift tax would be charged only on the value of the property when it is put into the trust ($400,000) and not on its appreciated value 20 years later ($1 million).

- No death taxes on the appreciated value.

- No probate.

52. CHARITABLE GIFTS AVOID DEATH TAXES.

Cash or property you give to charity during your life will be free of gift and death taxes and probate.

This is a simple idea not usually thought of as a method to reduce death taxes.

There are four major benefits to giving property to charity during your life:

- Doing something worthy.

- Avoidance of gift and death taxes.

- Avoidance of probate.

- Income tax deductions.

A CHARITABLE REMAINDER TRUST

STEP ONE:
You set up a charitable remainder trust.

→

STEP TWO:
You place appreciating property into the trust.

STEP THREE:
Your trust sells the property, with no income or capital-gains tax.

←

$1.2 million

→

STEP FOUR:
Your trust provides you with up to 10 percent income for life.

$10,000 a month to you

STEP FIVE:
On your death, your property goes to charity, death-tax free.

CHARITIES
OF YOUR CHOICE

CHURCH
HOSPITAL
SCHOOL

ORGANIZATION
SOCIETY
RESEARCH

53. CHARITABLE REMAINDER TRUSTS AVOID DEATH TAXES.

You can avoid death taxes and receive income tax deductions with a charitable remainder trust.

"**F**red" was unmarried and childless. He owned properties valued over $3 million, from which he earned an income of $75,000 a year. His will left his properties to his church.

Because of the size of his income, Fred did not want to give any of his properties away during his life. He didn't want to sell the properties because the proceeds would be subject to capital gains. Yet, he also wanted to increase his income.

Placing nearly all his properties into a charitable remainder trust was ideal for Fred for several reasons:

- No probate.

- The trust could sell the properties and pay Fred the income from the proceeds.

- No capital gains on sales by the trust.

- Fred's annual income from the trust would be about 10 percent — $300,000.

- Fred would receive charitable deductions which would increase his net income.

- After death, his church would get the properties.

A FAMILY FOUNDATION

STEP ONE:
You set up a
family foundation.

→

STEP TWO:
Your foundation
donates money
annualy to charity.

✝ **CHARITIES** ✝
OF YOUR CHOICE

CHURCH	ORGANIZATION
HOSPITAL	SOCIETY
SCHOOL	RESEARCH

STEP THREE:
You receive income
from the foundation
and tax deductions
for your life.

INCOME
& TAX
DEDUCTIONS
FOR LIFE

↓

STEP FOUR:
After your death
your heirs can
continue to manage
and receive income
from the foundation
indefinitely.

INCOME
& TAX
DEDUCTIONS
INDEFINITELY

54. FAMILY CHARITABLE FOUNDATIONS AVOID DEATH TAXES.

You can easily save death taxes and provide income for your heirs after your death with your own family charitable foundation.

Well known family charitable foundations include the Ford and Rockefeller Foundations. However, you don't have to be rich to benefit from such a foundation.

Indeed, with only a modest donation, your foundation can not only benefit charity, but can provide unlimited future employment for your heirs in managing your foundation long after your death. Unlike non-charitable trusts, your foundation can last indefinitely in the future.

To assess the benefits of such a foundation, see your estate-planning attorney.

55. BENEFICIARIES OF DEPENDENT PLANS AVOID DEATH TAXES.

Social security and other death benefit or annuity plans going directly to your beneficiaries are death-tax free.

You can easily set up death benefit or annuity plans for your beneficiaries which are free of death taxes.

Some plans include social security benefits, employer-paid annuities and death-benefit plans.

It is important for you to know these plans exist and to take advantage of them if they are available to you. Your estate-planning attorney can assist you.

56. LEAVE UP TO $1 MILLION TO GRANDCHILDREN TAX FREE.

You can leave up to $1 million to your grandchildren death-tax free with a generation-skipping trust.

This is one of those complicated areas of estate planning that only benefits the wealthy who want to leave a great deal of property to their grandchildren and avoid death taxes and probate.

You should ask your attorney whether this device would benefit your estate.

57. LIFE INSURANCE CAN AVOID DEATH TAXES.

You can easily provide your heirs with life insurance proceeds free of death taxes.

"**J**ack," a caller on my radio talk show, proudly told me he had purchased $1 million in life insurance which he claimed would be free of probate and death taxes.

"Can you change the beneficiaries of your policy?" I asked.

"Sure," Jack replied, "anytime I want."

"Then," I said, "your policy may avoid probate, but it will be subject to death taxes."

In Chapter 15, I recommended you purchase life insurance as a strategy to avoid probate.

Life insurance can also avoid death taxes. However, there are some strict requirements for this to work.

For life insurance to be free of death taxes, you must give up ownership, the right to change the beneficiaries and the right to borrow against your policy, and your estate must not be a beneficiary of the insurance.

Be careful. Life insurance can avoid death taxes, but only if your policy complies with death-tax laws.

58. TRANSFERS BY ANNUITY AVOID DEATH TAXES.

You can reduce death and income taxes and avoid probate by selling income-producing property for an annuity paid to you.

This is a strategy that sounds more complicated than it is.

A transfer by annuity is usually the sale of income-producing property between family members in return for lifetime annual payments.

How can this strategy save you income and death taxes? Simple.

- **It saves income taxes** because you apportion the sales price over a period of years.

- **It saves death taxes** and avoids probate by removing the income-producing asset from your estate.

Because of some unique pitfalls regarding a sale by annuity, it is highly recommended that you get legal advice on the costs and benefits of this strategy before using it.

A TYPICAL INSTALLMENT SALE

STEP ONE:
You transfer real estate to your child for fair value.

STEP TWO:
Your child pays you monthly installments for life.

STEP THREE:
If you die before all installments are paid, the debt is wiped out and the property avoids death taxes and probate.

TAX & PROBATE FREE

59. TRANSFERS BY INSTALLMENT AVOID DEATH TAXES.

A transfer by installment note can reduce income and death taxes and avoid probate.

This is another strategy that sounds more complicated than it is.

A transfer by installment note is the sale of any property with the payments made over time. Most people transfer the property to their heirs.

How can this strategy save you income and death taxes?

• **It saves income taxes** because 60 percent of the annual payments can be considered the return of principal (your original investment in the property). A return of principal is not taxed. That can save you a lot of income taxes.

• **It saves death taxes** and avoids probate by getting the property out of your estate. If the property appreciates by the time of your death, the transfer saves death taxes on the appreciation.

A SALE AND LEASE BACK

STEP ONE:
You sell your
business to your
child for fair value.

STEP TWO:
You lease the
business back
from your child.

STEP THREE:
After you die, the business is out of your
estate and the property avoids death taxes
and probate.

TAX &
PROBATE
FREE

60. SALE AND LEASE BACK AVOID DEATH TAXES.

A sale and lease back can reduce income and death taxes and avoid probate.

Again, this is a strategy that sounds more complicated than it is.

A sale and lease back is a sale between family members of a business and a lease back of the business by the seller.

How can this strategy save you income and death taxes?

It can save income taxes because the seller can deduct payments made to the buyer.

It can also save death taxes if you sell a business that appreciates to a family member.

Why? Because between the time of sale and the time of your death, the business will have appreciated. But only the original (and presumably lower) sales price is subject to death taxes.

61. QTIP TRUSTS AVOID DEATH TAXES.

*A QTIP trust allows you to postpone payment
of death taxes on your property until
after your spouse dies. It's also known
as an "anti-new spouse" provision.*

A QTIP is not something you buy at the corner drug store to clean your ears. It means "Qualified Terminable Interest Property." It is a trust permitted by the IRS Code which allows you to postpone the payment of death taxes on your property until after your spouse dies.

Also known as an "anti-new spouse" provision, a QTIP can prevent Fifi Lamour from disinheriting your children by giving her only income for life and preserving your property for your children.

There are special rules regarding such a trust and you should discuss its advantages and disadvantages with your attorney.

62. WHAT IS THE THREE-YEAR RULE?

A gift made within three years of death is included in your estate for purposes of imposing a death tax. You can easily avoid this rule by early planning.

Under the IRS Code, any gift you make within three years of your death is automatically included in your estate to impose the death tax. The gift is not cancelled. Its value is just included in your gross estate.

How do you avoid the Three-Year Rule?

DO NOT PROCRASTINATE.

Do your estate planning now. Read this book. See your attorney and/or trust company. Have your will and trusts drawn up.

Do not delay. In estate planning, even one day of delay can needlessly cost your estate tens or hundreds of thousands of dollars.

E. DISABILITY AND DEATH WITH DIGNITY

Don't be a menace to society.

TYPICAL DURABLE POWER OF ATTORNEY LANGUAGE

The following are examples of the language used in typical durable power of attorney forms.

- **When you want your power of attorney to become effective only after you become disabled:**

> THIS POWER OF ATTORNEY SHALL BECOME EFFECTIVE UPON MY DISABILITY OR INCAPACITY AND IS VALID UNTIL MY SAID ATTORNEY HAS ACTUAL KNOWLEDGE OF MY REVOCATION OF THE POWER IN WRITING OR MY DEATH.

- **When you want your power of attorney to be effective now:**

> THIS POWER OF ATTORNEY SHALL NOT BE AFFECTED BY DISABILITY OR INCAPACITY AND IS VALID UNTIL MY SAID ATTORNEY HAS ACTUAL KNOWLEDGE OF MY REVOCATION OF THE POWER IN WRITING OR MY DEATH.

If you have executed a general or special power of attorney, but language similar to the above does not appear anywhere on its face, **you do not have a durable power of attorney!**

63. DO YOU NEED A DURABLE POWER OF ATTORNEY?

*A durable power of attorney is an easy way
to appoint someone in advance to be
your guardian should you
become incapacitated.*

At a deposition, A. James Casner, the renowned Harvard professor and author of a treatise on estate planning, leaned forward and asked the attorney questioning him, "Have you got a durable power of attorney?"

"No," The startled attorney replied, "I don't."

"You're stupid then," snapped Professor Casner, "anybody in this room that doesn't have a (durable) power of attorney [is] a menace to society" because "you could be hit on the head and lie in a coma and all your affairs would be tied up."

Without a durable power of attorney, a guardianship must be established to handle your financial affairs. What's wrong with that? Plenty. You need to hire an attorney and ask a court to appoint a guardian. The guardian may well be a stranger to you. The proceeding is public and takes a lot of time. And it is very expensive.

In most states, a durable power of attorney performs all the functions of a guardian. It has many advantages. It is cheap, easy to prepare and private. It doesn't involve the courts. And you choose your own guardian.

So don't be a "menace to society"—prepare a durable power of attorney.

TYPICAL LIVING WILL

The following is an example of the language used in a typical living will.

If at any time I should have an incurable or irreversible condition certified to be terminal by two physicians who have personally examined me, one of whom shall be my attending physician, and the physicians have determined that I am unable to make decisions concerning my medical treatment, and that without administration of life-sustaining treatment my death will occur in a relatively short time, and where the application of life-sustaining procedures would serve only to prolong artificially the dying process, I direct that such procedures be withheld or withdrawn, and that I be permitted to die naturally with only the administration of medication, nourishment, or fluids or the performance of any medical procedure deemed necessary to provide me with comfort or to alleviate pain.

In the absence of my ability to give directions regarding the use of such life-sustaining procedures, it is my intention that this declaration shall be honored by my family and physician(s) as the final expressions of my legal right to refuse medical or surgical treatment and accept the consequences from such refusal.

The following is a provision I use for an unmarried mate to be treated as a family member:

It is further my desire that if at any time I should be hospitalized or institutionalized JANE DOE shall have full access to my medical records, to visit me, to receive medical information about me from my physician, to participate in decisions about my medical care and to be treated as a member of my family.

64. DO YOU NEED A LIVING WILL?

Your living will directs your doctor to allow you to die a natural death and that your life not be prolonged by machines.

We have all heard the tragic stories of patients such as Karen Anne Quinlan lingering in a coma on life support machines for days, months and even years.

Why? Under the Hippocratic Oath, physicians are morally, ethically and legally obligated to prolong life. They feel they have a duty to keep people alive, even on machines.

A "living will" allows you to die a natural death. It directs your physician not to use artificial means to prolong your life where there is no reasonable expectation of survival and to administer only nourishment and pain medications.

For unmarried couples, have your attorney include a clause that directs your physician to treat your designated "significant other" as a member of your family. This will ensure your unmarried mate has rights of visitation and consultation with your physician.

TYPICAL FORM FOR SIGNING DOCUMENT WITH AN "X"

IN WITNESS WHEREOF, I have set my hand at the city of _____, State of _____, this _____ day of _____, 19__.

_____
SAM BENNETT

The mark near the written name of SAM BENNETT was made by SAM BENNETT as his signature in my presence, he stating he made his mark as his signature. At his request, I wrote his name to the right of that mark and wrote my name below.

_____
JIM JONES

Signed, published, and declared by SAM BENNETT, as and for his (will, durable power of attorney, living will, trust, etc). SAM BENNETT, being unable to write his name made his mark, after which JIM JONES signed the name of SAM BENNETT near the mark and wrote his own name as witness to the mark in the presence of us, all being present at the same time, and who at SAM BENNETT's request, in his presence and in the presence of each other have signed our names as witnesses on the above date. We certify SAM BENNETT is in our opinions and beliefs of sound and disposing mind and memory.

_____   _____
WITNESS   WITNESS

65. IF YOU CAN ONLY SIGN WITH AN "X".

You can sign your durable power of attorney, will, living will, trust or other legal documents with an "X," even if someone else has to assist you to do it.

"**S**am Bennett" was afflicted with Parkinson's Disease which attacked his nerves, precluding voluntary control of his muscles.

His mind was sound and he could understand the consequences of legal documents such as a durable power of attorney, will, living will or trust. However, he could no longer walk, talk or sign his name without assistance.

Would Sam's afflictions preclude him from executing an estate plan? Of course not!

Sam is permitted to sign any any legal document with an "X." If he is unable to sign an "X" by himself, he can be assisted by a second person such as his wife. The signature must be witnessed by the minimum number required by the laws of his state.

The prior page has a typical form for witnesses to acknowledge having observed Sam sign a legal document with the assistance of his wife, Joan Bennett. A neighbor, Jim Jones wrote Sam's name next to his "X."

66. HOW YOU CAN DONATE ORGANS.

You can easily donate your body or portions of it to a medical school or transplant facility.

Every state has passed the Uniform Anatomical Gift Act which allows you to donate all or part of your body for research or for transplantation. You can include a clause in your will that designates what you want to do regarding donation of organs.

F. CHOOSING YOUR ESTATE-PLANNING ATTORNEY

Don't be penny wise and pound foolish.

67. HOW YOU CAN FIND AN ESTATE-PLANNING ATTORNEY.

You deserve the best there is — so get an experienced estate-planning attorney to prepare your plan.

Every person in need of an attorney asks the same question, "Where do I find a good one?"

I have a simple three-step method of selection:

- **Step one:** Do groundwork. Ask your friends for recommendations. Check with the bar association and the yellow pages for lists of attorneys specializing in estate planning. Compile a list of three or four whose names are most frequently recommended.

- **Step two:** Interview the attorneys. Determine how experienced they are. How long they have practiced estate planning? How many wills and trusts have they prepared? How much do they charge?

- **Step three:** Select the attorney. Base your selection on his experience and your comfort in his ability to communicate and understand your situation. Cost is important, but see the next chapter for cost considerations.

68. WHAT WILL AN ESTATE PLAN COST?

In the long-run, an estate plan will save your estate tens or hundreds of thousands of dollars.

Among the most frequent questions I am asked are:

- "How much does a will cost?"

- "How much does a trust cost?"

- "How much does an estate plan cost?"

These are legitimate questions. But there is no easy answer to each question. It doesn't cost very much money to prepare a simple will or trust or print a living will from a computer.

It can, however, take a lot of time to do the appropriate amount of estate plannning for your estate. It all boils down to how complex it is. A simple revocable living trust, will, living will, and durable power of attorney, for example, might cost you no more than $1,000. However, to create a proper plan may cost a lot more.

The ultimate issue is not whether you can afford an estate plan, but whether you can afford not to do everything you can to avoid probate, reduce death taxes and ensure your heirs receive 100 percent of everything to which they are entitled under the law.

Don't be penny wise and pound foolish. Spend what is necessary to ensure that your estate receives all the planning it deserves. In the long run, your estate will save several times more in death taxes and probate costs than the cost of preparing your plan.

DEFINITIONS

Estate planning terms are defined in the chapters of this book. However, to help you, I have also prepared the following glossary. To the best of my ability, I have tried to define these terms in plain language and not "legalese."

Annuity sale: there are many kinds of annuities; for estate planning, this refers to the sale of income-producing property between family members in exchange for lifetime annual payments.

Appreciating property: property, such as real estate, valuable paintings or old coins, which increases in value over time.

Bank account trust: a trust which specifies who is to receive the funds in your bank account upon your death; known as a "Totten Trust."

Beneficiary: someone entitled to a portion of your estate, either by law or as directed by you in your will, trust, life insurance policy, or retirement program.

Charitable remainder trust: an irrevocable trust with an IRS-approved charity as the beneficiary; you receive the income from the trust for life; after death, the assets in the trust go to charity.

Charity: donations to an IRS-approved charity are generally death- and income-tax free.

Codicil: a document which amends a will.

Death tax: see estate tax.

Disability insurance: insurance which covers you during a period of disability.

Durable power of attorney: a power of attorney effective even after you have become mentally or physically incompetent or incapacitated; saves the expense and time delays of a court hearing to appoint a guardian to handle your affairs.

Estate: all the property you own at your death.

Estate tax: the federal government and most state governments impose a tax on the value of your estate; gift and estate tax rates are equal; also known as the death tax.

Estate tax exclusion: the amount of property free of death taxes; see "lifetime estate tax credit" and "marital estate tax exclusion."

Executor: the person named by you in your will to handle the probate of your estate; also known as the "personal representative."

Family charitable foundation: a foundation set up by you to benefit charity; your heirs can be designated the managers of the foundation from which they receive income.

Generation-skipping trust: a device to leave property to your grandchildren which exempts up to $1 million in death taxes.

Gift: the transfer of property with no remuneration; gifts can avoid death taxes and probate.

Gift tax: the federal government imposes a tax on any gift you make over $11,000 per person each year; the gift and death tax rates are the same.

Gift tax exclusion: you pay no gift tax on gifts up to $11,000 per person per year; see definition of "gift tax."

Grantor retained income trust: also known as a GRIT; a trust which allows you to get appreciating property out of your estate to reduce death taxes.

Guardian: a person appointed by a court to handle your financial and business affairs if you become mentally or physically incapacitated; see "durable power of attorney."

Installment sales: a sale by installment note with the payments paid over time; this strategy can be used to save death taxes.

Intestate: to die without a will; if you die without a will, the laws of your state will determine who gets your estate.

Inter vivos trust: a revocable or irrevocable trust set up during your lifetime.

Irrevocable family trust: a trust which cannot be revoked or amended; it can be set up during your life (called an "inter vivos trust") or by your will (called a "testamentary trust").

Joint tenancy: a form of ownership of property under which the surviving owner obtains complete title to the property after you die; joint tenancy avoids probate, but has many disadvantages; see "tenancy by the entireties."

Life insurance: insurance payable to your beneficiaries on your death; if you give up ownership of your policy and your estate is not a beneficiary, the policy is free of death taxes and probate.

Lifetime estate-tax credit: you can leave to your heirs up to $1 million free of death and gift taxes; also known as the "unified credit;" you can also leave an unlimited amount to your spouse free of death and gift taxes (see "marital death tax exclusion").

Living will: a document by which you direct your physician, after he determines you are terminally ill, to remove life support machines and to administer only nourishment and pain medications.

Marital death-tax exclusion: any property left to your spouse is free of death and gift taxes.

Personal representative: the person appointed by the court to supervise the probate of your estate, especially if you die without a will or fail to name an executor in your will; see "executor."

Per capita: Inheritance in one's "own right."

Per stirpes: Inheritance by "right of representation."

Pour-over will: the transfer of your property after death from your will to your trust.

Power of attorney: grants another person the right to act in your place; a "special" power of attorney grants the right to perform a specific task described in the document; a "general" power of attorney grants the right to do anything you could; see "durable power of attorney."

Pretermitted heir: a natural or adopted child intentionally or accidentally omitted from your will; most states allow an omitted natural, adopted or illegitimate child to claim a percentage of your estate.

Probate: the court proceeding which transfers your estate to your heirs.

QTIP Trust: QTIP stands for "qualified terminable interest property;" it is a trust that delays death taxes until after the second spouse dies.

Revocable living trust: a trust made during your lifetime which can be changed, revoked or amended at any time.

Rule against perpetuities: the rule prevents you from setting up a trust to last forever. It only allows you to tie up property for a period of 21 years after the death of someone living at your death.

Sale and lease back: a sale between family members of a business and a lease back of the business by the seller; this strategy can be used to reduce death and income taxes.

Settlor: a person who sets up a trust.

Simultaneous death clause: Permits you to state in your will to whom your property will go if you and your spouse die in a common calamity.

Tenancy by the entireties: joint tenancy of any property by a married couple; see "joint tenancy."

Tenants in common: a form of ownership of property which you can leave to anyone you designate in your will or trust; unlike joint tenancy, the surviving tenant does not automatically inherit the property and it does not avoid probate.

Testamentary trust: a trust created by your will and effective after you die.

Testator/testatrix: the name of a man or woman, respectively, who set up a will of their estate.

Three-Year Rule: gifts made within three years of death are included in your estate for purposes of imposing a death tax.

Totten Trust: see "bank account trust."

Transfer by annuity: see "annuity sale."

Transfer by installment: see "installment sale."

Trust: a document which entrusts you or another person with your property for the benefit of you or someone else; see "revocable living trust," "irrevocable family trust," "testamentary trust," "inter vivos trust," "grantor retained income trust," "QTIP trust," "Totten trust" and "generation-skipping trust."

Trustee: the person(s) named by you to manage your trust; during your life, you can be your own trustee of your revocable living trust.

Unified credit: see "lifetime death tax credit."

Uniform Anatomical Gift Act: the law which allows you to donate all or part of your body or organs for research or for transplantation.

Will: a document which, among other things, directs who will get your estate upon your death, who will administer your estate in probate and who will be the guardian of your minor children.

INDEX

Order More Books
It's
Fast, Easy, and Inexpensive

If You Die Tomorrow
Just $10 plus $1.50 postage/handling per book.
Mail check or money order for $11.50 per book to:

**Lilly & Associates
PO Box 3439
Honolulu, HI 96801-3439**

Order Michael Lilly's New Video

Understanding Estate Planning is *Easy*

Michael Lilly's new video is 40+ minutes. Once you see it you'll understand probate and why you should avoid it, all about death taxes and how to avoid them, and more importantly, why it is so easy and imperative that you get a living trust. Send your check or money order today and Michael (his secretary really) will send you a copy of the video **Understanding Estate Planning Is *Easy*.**

Understanding Estate Planning Is *Easy*
Just $19.95 plus $2.55 postage/handling per video.
(The retail price is $39.95 plus tax).

Mail check or money order for $22.50 per video to the address listed above.

**Make check or money order to: Lilly & Associates
Sorry, no credit card orders**